Huh,

and other deep thoughts

By L. Phillips Carlson

Huh, and other deep thoughts
By L. Phillips Carlson

Published by
SnowSnake Press
PO Box 51732
Albuquerque NM 87181

Also available on Kindle and other devices
Printed by CreateSpace

Cover credits, interior design and illustrations:
L. Phillips Carlson

Acknowledgements

I would be remiss if I didn't mention my good friends who are also great writers: Kathlena L. Contreras (K. Lynn Bay) and Lara LaVonne Jordan. Thank you for all your help and support!

I'd also like to thank the Asbury United Methodist Church family (Albuquerque) for all those years I edited their newsletter and experimented on them with my various homilies.

Thanks, especially, to my family, who gets portrayed more often than they'd like, I'm sure.

And thanks to my talented sister, Dr. Tamara Fudge, who designed my website and keeps it going so professionally: http://lphillipscarlson.com.

Couldn't do this without all of you!

Contents

Huh—a forward

Hi there! I decided to put several of my pieces and poems that were written over the years in a little book that I hope you'll enjoy. I'm picturing myself sitting in a coffee shop with you, chatting and sharing life's joys, sorrows, and oddities. I used to be a church newsletter editor, so several of the selections in here reflect my own particular faith. But I think the experiences I've had are likely similar to yours, whatever your beliefs are. Sometimes we need something greater than ourselves to lean on.

Many of these selections have been previously published in various places. I'm including a list at the end of the book if you're interested. I've heavily edited everything, though, for this version—mostly because I'm a better writer now!

And some of this is brand new, including "Getting Ready," a piece I sold. Unfortunately, the magazine went under before it was published.

I've been accused of being somewhat of a philosopher, but I can't take myself too seriously. These are coffee-klatch type thoughts, so that's why I chose the title I did. Maybe one will strike you as more meaningful—a lady I know put "One Wrong Note" on her refrigerator because she liked it so much—but mostly, I'm just expecting a thoughtful "huh" out of you.

Feel free to visit my website and send me comments: http://lphillipscarlson.com.

Happy reading!

On Renewal

Mended

I do not sew, except under protest. It's a skill I simply do not enjoy.

But recently, I needed a skirt to go with an outfit, and I couldn't find anything in the stores that was the right color or a reasonable price. So I gathered my courage and set out to a fabric store, hunting for something suitable. Finally, armed with yardage and instructions that promised "2-hour pattern," I launched into my project.

Six hours later, my patience was raveling nearly as fast as the seam allowances. But the skirt was almost done.

Then I did it. Instead of clipping the thread, I caught a small bit of the fabric and cut a hole in my brand-new, custom-made skirt.

I couldn't believe I did that! After I quit moaning, though, I noticed that the hole was in an area with a lot of fullness. So I grabbed a needle and thread and put in a few wobbly stitches from underneath. Thankfully, the pattern was forgiving and the skirt's folds hid my flaw.

That episode made me grateful that no one was around to hear me carry on! It also made me think about all the flaws we keep hidden, parts of ourselves we don't like—like my bad mood. Sometimes our very souls could use a little mending.

Fortunately, in the fullness of God's forgiveness, we are made whole again. We are sewn from the underside with grace and love so that we are solid once more. Given a chance to heal and transform into our better selves, we no longer need to be full of unmended holes.

∂∽∕

The Feast

(an ode to my choirs)

The hungry souls gather,
their essence tattered and piecemeal
after the long week's toil,
each with painful bits wrenched away
by work, by home, by life itself.
They come,
with tears and lightless eyes,
but with hope and desire
for renewal.

Some search in earnest prayer
or in solitude,
some in the quiet sympathy of a friend's ear.
But all come here
to be healed again
by the unseen power
of the music.

Their unfettered demand resounds
until a tornado fills the room.

Undaunted, the conductor stirs the pot of
fragmented spirits,
faster and faster,
lassoing strays with a sharp snap of words.
With horns or halo, he coaxes them
and draws them out of the soup.
They cling to his baton
as he twists them, tighter and tighter
into a single golden rope—
the errant vitality, now finely spun,
a miracle of shared harmony.

The singers drink deeply of the lyrical nectar,
their resonance filling each other's gaps
with the glue of creativity.
And when it stops,
they are full,
able to face the ravenous world,
knowing that
another repast awaits them
next week.

෧෧

Letting Go

One of my pastors had a sermon series about having "enough," which reminded me of our family's worst pet—a hamster. His name was Squirt, because of what he did when you held him, and he was grumpy and did nothing but eat and poop. But he did manage to hoard extra food and treats in all the corners of his habitat, making impressive piles sometimes, especially when we forgot to clean the cage.

Unfortunately, we humans aren't much better than Squirt as far as hoarding goes. I read in the news recently that hoarding is considered a psychological disorder if it actually gives you pain to get rid of "stuff." Oops. I think many of us qualify.

My sister and I cleaned out my mother's house after she relocated to my town, and I can tell you my mom is a true Depression-era kid who never threw away anything remotely useful. It took us a month, all told, which I understand is pretty typical. But before I can chastise anyone, I have to take a good, long look at my own house. Yeah, my husband and I are going through the garage and the drawers and closets, slowly but surely. I don't want to leave a huge mess to my own kids—but it's a continual process, a constant battle against clutter and accumulation. Maybe I ought to apologize to them in advance.

As we've sorted, we've found knick-knacks that we sort of remember, but can't tell why we have them or why they were once important. So, out they go! Other things seem less vibrant or useful than when we got them. Those get donated. And some stuff—why would anyone have bags of old rags or ancient magazines?—simply go in the trash or recycle bin.

I thought about my current "collection" of stuff. It seems that, like old clothes, we outgrow things. If we hang on to too much, it makes it impossible to grow and change and keep moving on in life. My husband and I have changed quite a bit from when we first married, so many years ago. It seems like our home and its furnishings should reflect our current selves rather than our former ones.

If I see my life as a flowing river, I can't hold on to too much or I'll sink like a rock. But if I let things come and go—or just let go entirely—God will keep me afloat and on track to the next change of scenery, to the next phase of life.

రుడ్యోళ్

Wild Hair

I've always envied
        those with wild hair.
You know the kind:
        thick-thought tresses
        with fat, curly notions,
        mane-like, full of
        ideas of their own,
        barely tamed enough to
        be rooted in the same scalp.
My non-persuasive hair is limp and fine,
        world-weary thin, smooth from routine
        and boringly flat.
People tell me
        the few stray hairs that
        dare to speak out
        are usually gray
        and not too exciting.
Oh, I've tried to fix my hair:
        I copied styles
        from all the magazines.
I even had others color or perm it,
        and give it their idea
        of wild hair.

But it never looked right,
        never fit,
        never was me.
So today I purged my hair with
        the shampoo of self.
I cleansed it layer by layer,
        and removed the debris of
        everyone else's preconceptions.
Then I dried it with conviction
        and looked hard in the mirror.
Guess what?
My hair is wild, too—
        a bit frizzy, perhaps,
        but wild nonetheless.
I see stubborn strands
        with definite opinions
        and finger-curl concepts
        with a lofty fullness.
And standing with comb in hand,
        I realize now
        that I have
        only myself to blame
        for combing it straight.

☙❧

On
Awe

F/X

"F/X," as I'm sure many of you know, is Hollywood shorthand for "special effects." It's exciting to go to the movies and experience spectacular train wrecks, jump into 3-D animated scenes, or crash-land a flying saucer on an alien planet. With a huge theater screen and surround-sound, we lose ourselves for an hour or two, feeling the thrills and chills as if we were actually there. The big picture swallows us up and carries us along for the ride.

A few years ago, my family and I went to the Grand Canyon, where we saw special effects of a different sort. We perched ourselves on a viewing promontory, surrounded by a serpentine part of the canyon itself. It was dusk and the spring air threatened to chill us to the bone. But we waited patiently, with camera and tripod, for the live showing of the sunset.

And quietly, without background music or other heralding, the colors of the yellow and brown walls yielded to successions of orange, pink and red. A hush fell over fellow tourists as we all watched in awe. It was as if an invisible brush were stroking the canyon with watercolor paint, continually changing from hue to delicate hue, until at last the dusty purple of night set in.

Watching the beauty transforming around me, my own importance suddenly shrank. But somehow, I belonged to this big picture, and I thanked God for including me. It was a thrill to sense something so much greater than myself, to see in person the artistry and splendor of his nature.

In our busy world, it's difficult to find the time and space to experience such quiet greatness. But it's there, with vast and wonderful special effects, if only we take the time to look.

જ‍ન્ય

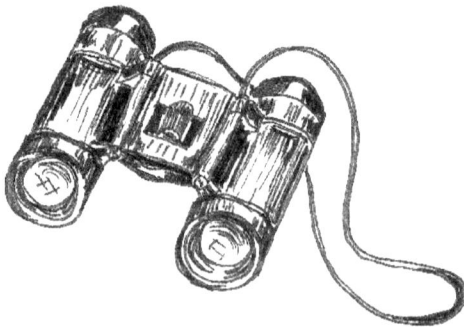

Harbinger

I saw a smudge of purple
Risen above the dreary winter gray:
A fragile crocus, all alone,
Bravely proclaiming impending spring,
While the weather, ever fickle,
Sat stonily undecided.
Such a small thing, just a bit of color,
Yet enough to make me pause
And smile, and remember
That better times and seasons are to come.

Just as a glimmer of dawn
Lightens the depression of night,
Just as a little ray of sunny hope
Makes storms pass from a drizzly world,
The modest man from Galilee
Gave us a glimpse of life's eternity
Shining as God's Son.
When all seemed dead as winter,
A tiny sprout of faith arose
And blossomed to full flower.
It was Life—Unsuppressed.

❧❧

Shadows and Light

It's a big universe. There are billions of galaxies made of even more stars, and it's anybody's guess how many planets like ours lie out there. The Earth is just one tiny speck in the larger scheme of things, barely worth mentioning.

I feel very small some days.

Yet, some time ago, we saw a lunar eclipse. That's when the Earth moves between the sun and the moon and casts a shadow on the moon. Our lunar neighbor took on an eerie, orange-red glow during the process. At other times, it looked like some unknown sky-monster had taken a huge bite out of it. Maybe you saw it too, or maybe you were watching night-time TV instead. It was a silent, strange thing, and easy to miss.

Then I suddenly realized that it was our shadow that covered the moon. Our little planet of space dust and debris was mighty enough to cast a shadow! A shadow means there is something solid sitting in the light. We do have substance—we do matter!

It made me feel very important.

It's easy to get lost in the universe of the everyday world and its galaxies of problems. Many of us just quietly go about helping others and do our best to be good citizens. Yet, in doing so, we stand in the light of our faith and that makes shadows. We do have an effect on those around us, even if it is an easy-to-miss thing.

And on frustrating cloudy days, I try to remember that shadows are strongest when standing in full Son.

∂∞⌐

Private Showing

It's magic early,
Not quite day.
Sh! Don't wake them yet.
Slipper into the sleeping world,
And look with pajama'ed eyes
At the water-colored realm.
Wide, low stripes of baby blanket sky
Fade into the far horizon;
The eastern glow begins.
Eyebrow clouds of dark blue feathers
Turn pink before advancing rays.
Wispy shadows now flame yellow
As the burn of day erases the night
One relentless color at a time.
Elusive, ever-changing Dawn,
Such a short appearance!
Too soon,
It's morning.

❧✧

October Woods

Crunch, crunch, crunch.
Autumn under my shoes.
The color riot drops
From unruly trees,
Withering and fading
To brown dullness.
Cool, crisp air in gentle breezes
Sharpen mood and mind,
Prickling a certain
Cold foreboding.
Freshly-picked apples
Tease my tongue
With a sharp tang,
A fleeting pleasure.
Between the baring branches
Lazy sun shines golden,
Mocking, for soon it
Departs
As howling winds
Etch dark
Silhouettes against
Grey skies.
Winter,
Coming.

On Forgive-ness

Clean Sweep

The other day I was stewing about some crass comments an acquaintance had made. This guy doesn't really see me the way I am, I thought, or he'd treat me with more respect. He'd know I was charming, witty, intelligent (just keep adding adjectives here).

Of course, I never make crass comments. Well, not *that* crass, anyway. OK, I admit that I didn't say anything very mean *that one time*.

I was still sure I'd been terribly wronged.

Later one of my friends stopped by for a quick chat. She told me she'd been doing a little "housekeeping" with her faith this week, and she felt great. I asked her specifically what she'd done.

"I forgave everybody for everything," she answered. "My parents, the difficult college prof—even the girls who tormented me in grade school. After all, if Jesus could forgive the people who tortured him, why can't I forgive those who did so much less to me?"

I stared at her calm and happy face, and realized that this was exactly what I needed to do: to forgive and go on, to drop all those emotional burdens. And while I was at it, I should probably ask some forgiveness for myself. It was all so simple.

And so hard.

People have been created with so many different personalities! There will always be some that will prove difficult for us. And yet, it's very freeing to just let go and give the problem to a higher power to solve.

So, instead of resolving to spring-clean all the corners of my house (or autumn-clean, which is the case when I'm writing this), I'm going to try to wash all the closets of my memory with forgiveness. It will not be easy, but it's something I have to do. And like pasting a picture of a thinner me on the refrigerator, I'm going to imprint in my mind's eye the image of my friend's serene face to help keep me on task.

❧❦

One Wrong Note

The concert was going well. Our choir sang with a confidence found only in the last few rehearsals. We began a difficult passage we'd gone over and over and perfected. I carefully counted and sang the odd rhythm with practiced ease. Even so, I accidently came in one beat too early, my own voice the only sound coming from the stage.

I wanted to run off in shame, but we weren't finished. My face froze as I tried not to look guilty.

After I got home, I ranted about the silly mistake I'd made, even though friends in the front row insisted they hadn't heard me. I'd never made that mistake in rehearsal, how could I have done it in concert?

"OK, Mom," my daughter said calmly. "Besides that one measure, how was the rest of the concert?"

Her remark cut my groveling short. Of course, my tiny mistake had not made the concert less glorious. It had gone really well and the audience responded enthusiastically. I needed to forgive myself and go on.

In Colossians 3:13, Paul says "…Forgive as the Lord forgave you." Not only are we to forgive others who wrong us, we are to forgive ourselves. But how difficult that is! We are our own worst critics, and spend too much time worrying about small errors. We are human after all, and will make many mistakes. God knows this. He forgives us freely, again and again. By not dwelling on our mistakes, we can embrace the songs and joys of life.

Dear Lord, please help me to forgive myself as freely as you forgive me. Keep me from dwelling on one wrong note, and help me to live joyfully in your presence. *Amen.*

෨෧

On Faith and Hope

Close to Home

Do you remember Halley's Comet in the mid-1980s? My husband and I roused our then-small children hours before dawn and drove off on a fruitless chase, hoping to catch a clear glimpse of something great. It turned out to be a disappointing bit of fuzz, just barely visible above the horizon.

However, in mid-March of 1997, another comet flew close to the earth. The clock read a mere 5:15 a.m. when my early-rising spouse woke me up.

"The Hale-Bopp comet!" he said. "You've got to see it!"

I dragged my groggy body out of bed while he continued, "I thought I'd have to look for it with binoculars. But it's right out the front door. All I had to do was look up."

Sure enough, I stepped out and saw the comet just over the mountains that lie to the east of our city. The comet's fiery nucleus shone brighter than anything else in the night sky, and its delicate halo of gases trailed off in a most impressive tail.

I watched, captivated by the glory of this "star" shining in the east, and thought how easy it had been to see it. No grumpy kids or long car rides. All I grabbed for this journey was a bathrobe and slippers.

I remember several other times I've searched high and low and found what I wanted close to home. On a camping trip to Colorado, my husband and I set off early one morning to find some mule deer. We must have hiked three or four miles before we gave up. Upon returning to our tent, we found a couple of deer happily munching leaves only a few yards away.

My faith search seems to be following this pattern as well. I venture out into the world and listen and learn, but the most revealing moments happen in conversations with friends or in the stillness of prayer. Mind you, I've enjoyed the trip immensely. But I need to remember that God is right on my doorstep, shining the way when I need it.

ॐॐ

Hope

Soft as snow
Our words fall.
Gently,
Smoothly,
Until they drift downward
To fickle ears.
We plant words like seeds
— Lavishly —
And then wait to see
If any grow
At all.

∂∘∾

Listening to Your Father

I think I was a fairly typical teenager—no angel, certainly, but not too bad, either. Of course, from time to time, my parents needed to correct my behavior or attitude, and sometimes it was hard to get through the self-absorption that plagues all of us at that age.

My dad would tell a story—for the umpteenth time—about a mule driver having to hit his mule with a stick just to get its attention. I knew what he wanted—my own attention—but I'd cock one hip, fold my arms, and sulk at him through long, straight bangs. "Yes, Dad?"

Sorry to say, I haven't completely lost my stubbornness, but it is a little easier to get my attention these days. A comic strip, of all things, popped out at me the other day. A young mother was bemoaning her inadequacy at taking care of her newborn, voicing her fears of the future to a confidante. "You're damned if you do, damned if you don't," she said.

Her wise friend lay a hand on hers and said,

"Or you're blessed if you do, blessed if you don't."

The message hit me like the mule driver's stick. Successful living is all about attitude. A former pastor had told us to "walk like a child of the King." Another pastor urged us to "step forward in faith." Sure, life is messy and we will face challenges, both good and bad. Life can be downright scary. But we aren't alone—God is there to guide and help. We can confidently walk into the future, knowing we're blessed and loved, regardless of whether we take false steps or not. The point is not to be afraid to try.

So, this time, it took two preachers and a comic strip to get my attention. And this time, I'm listening.

ॐ⬥ॐ

One of Those 'God Things'

I knew a woman who used to attend my church before she moved back to Texas. When confronted with unusual happenings that turned out beneficially, she'd pronounce them as "one of those God things," and could not be persuaded otherwise.

Well, some time ago, I experienced one of those God things myself.

As usual, I had too much to do. I'm a member of a symphonic chorus, and one summer we took a trip to Vail, Colorado, to participate in a music festival there. We sang Beethoven's Ninth Symphony—with the Philadelphia Orchestra, no less—at a wonderful outdoor venue. The chorus sings at the very end, the lyrics taken from a German work, "*An die Freude*," (Ode to Joy). I'm sure you know the melody: it's the same one in the old hymn, "Joyful, Joyful, We Adore Thee."

Anyway, as a volunteer chorus, it was very exciting for us to be doing this, even if it meant a long, chartered bus ride both ways, exacting rehearsals, and taking time away from work and family.

It was also the time I needed to edit the next edition of the church newsletter, so I took my laptop with me. On the bus, I opened an e-mail from the associate pastor and started reading her article: "One of my favorite classical composers is Ludwig van Beethoven." *What an odd coincidence!* I thought. It went on to mention the joy he was able to convey even when he was going through the grief of being deaf. And the specific piece she cited was his Ninth Symphony, *the very one I was about to sing.*

I was stunned. The pastor, it turned out, had no clue that my chorus was performing it. More amazing still was her choice of Bible verses — Isaiah 55:12: *"For you shall go out in joy, and be led back in peace; the mountains and the hills before you shall burst into song, and all the trees of the field shall clap their hands."* As I stood onstage in the Gerald Ford Amphitheater in Vail, with mountains and hills and trees all around, this verse became all too real. The sold-out audience burst into enthusiastic applause and cheered at the end of our concert. The roar hit us like a clap of thunder.

I shared my pastor's words with many chorus friends and my director, and they were all astonished at the synchronicity. One woman was literally in tears after she read it. While the Ninth is an all-out, ebullient and exhausting exercise, the article made us remember its more spiritual meaning. Everything combined to make that performance one of the high points of my entire musical career.

I'm quite sure, though, when my Texan friend hears about this, that she won't be surprised at all. "Just one of those God things," she'll say.

❧

On
Sorrow

I Cry

I cry at your funeral, my friend,
But not for you.
You just lie there —
a gray imposter of what you used to be,
And a bad imitation at that.
The spark of you is gone;
I don't know where.

Your new stillness is frightening.
It's too quiet, too unreal.
I can't take it in.
I cry.

Outside,
There are blue skies and warm sun.
The world is strangely normal —
Cars pass, people bustle,
How can this be?
How dare they carry on
And ignore my suffering?
Does no one understand my pain?

I cry.

But I do not cry for you.
My life is changed;
I had no choice.
Your death reminds me
I am mortal and fragile;
I don't like that.
And worst of all,
You're not here to help me through this.
I feel alone, so alone.

I cry.

Stop, selfish tears!
They heed me not.
Then a thought pops in my weariness,
An amazing thought, weaving through the tears.
Suddenly, I understand.

I still cry.
And it's OK.
But I do not cry for you, my friend,
I cry for me.

ॐ

Missing You

You said hello
And pressed me close
In a warm embrace.
But, when you left,
You took it with you.

We laughed and smiled
And shared as friends.
But it's quiet now
For you had to say goodbye
And travel back to your other life —
The one without me.

꩜

unfettered

Ice-capped mountains
Behind black hills
Beckon to me;
I wonder still
How something so austere and cold
Could have so much appeal.

Craggy faces now appear
Where once a granite wall stood clear.
Oddly, they all look the same —
Nameless; yet I feel that pain
Of seeing you, again.

The sun grows faint;
And though I know
I should return from wind and snow,
I wait to hear their winter song
'Til bitter, callous end.

The fading stone turns melon pink;
And warmth and light begin to sink.
As cold night air assails and wakes,
And daylight dies in gloomy break,
My thoughts turn icy clear.

For like the dusk and mountain stone,
Your changing moods have deftly sewn
Sorry shadows on my heart.
From you, O haunted, darkened chill,
I gratefully depart.

ॐ

On Caring

Brown Jello

So many smiling faces and well-behaved children adorn the pages of magazines during the holidays. They seem to say that you, too, can create food worthy of a chef, make clever Martha Stewart décor, and wrap packages that Macy's would envy. In other words, you can have a "perfect" Christmas.

Yeah, right. If your Christmases are anything like mine, it's less Norman Rockwell and more unscripted You-tube.

For example, although I'm usually a pretty good cook, I can mess up grandly with simple stuff like Jello gelatin. Most years when the kids were growing up, I made a light dessert with distinct layers of red and green gelatin, separated by a creamy layer of Cool-Whip topping. "Christmas Jello," I called it. But a couple of times the layers flowed into each other, creating a cola-brown gunk of mixed cherry and lime flavors. We ate it anyway. To this day, I get teased about it, even though I managed to perfect it in succeeding years.

Our Christmas trees have often been less than perfect, too. One year we chose a sturdy piñon pine — a little too sturdy, it turned out. Its fat trunk didn't fit our usual stand, so I bought a new one, a strange contraption with chains and an industrial-looking water pan. It was a rather imposing tree, but served us well until after Christmas when we needed to take it down. It had relaxed so much that its stiff branches wouldn't fit through the doorway any more. We had to cut it apart right there in the living room—getting sawdust and sap all over—just to get it out of the house.

People haven't always been in the best of moods, either. There was the time that one of the kids told the other that Santa hadn't come (not true!), which elicited many anxious wails and cries, followed by someone getting sent to their room! We've been snowed in, had roof leaks with water pouring in on Christmas Eve, and had painstakingly, hand-folded luminarias blow away. One year, some presents were mixed-up—no tags—by a relative who swore she could remember what was in each box. It rapidly lost its humor after opening up the fourth box of someone else's underwear and socks.

But what the heck—we were together and weathered it all, and that was most important. Those brown Jello moments weren't disasters, they gave us a unique history as a family. Perfection, in my opinion, is overrated.

৵৵৶

All Their Fingers

One thing I've always appreciated about my church is that I could count on everyone to guide my kids. If my children misbehaved, some adult felt free to set them straight. And I've felt free to do the same to the other children.

I don't enjoy playing the role of the "crabby lady," but I realize it is part of my responsibility toward my church family.

I wish this would extend to the outside world as well. When I was growing up, neighbors, teachers and most other adults watched out for each other and for all the kids. People seem afraid to do this anymore, and sometimes with good reason. A disgruntled youth may be armed, or some lawyer-wielding child may slap you with a harassment suit.

Some time ago, I was standing at the counter of a copy shop, waiting for my order. A harried young mother rushed in with a darling little girl of about four years old. Realizing that she forgot the items she needed, the mom left the child alone in the store and dashed out to her car for a moment.

As kids will do when unsupervised, the blond-headed tot headed for the nearest toy-like item: in this case, an old-fashioned, guillotine-sharp paper cutter. She proceeded to cut tiny scraps of paper with it, her little fingers only millimeters from the savage blade.

I immediately pointed her out to the counter clerk. He shook his head, as if to say, "Gee, that's too bad," but did nothing. I found this incredible, since his store could be sued if she hurt herself. A couple of other adult bystanders noticed the child's actions, but similarly did nothing.

I looked at the young innocent. She might want to play piano or guitar someday, and certainly she'd use a computer keyboard. Surely, she'd want all of her fingers.

I hurried over to the child, carefully closed the blade, and said in my sternest voice, "I'm sorry, you can't use this. This is only for grown-ups."

The mother returned at this time and heard me. She sprang to her child's side and ungratefully said, "Well! I don't think she hurt it," meaning the cutter. She was completely clueless about the danger.

Her remark stung and I felt badly, but I'm not sorry I did it. I can empathize with the mom, weary from constant vigilance to the point of not thinking straight. I can only hope I was more gracious when strangers interfered for my children's safety.

It's hard to take our guiding eyes out of a consenting group like our home church, but we should gently look for opportunities. If we follow our faith's teachings, some young people may be grateful someday for their values, their manners, or maybe all their fingers.

Keeping Statistics

Soccer is a great game to watch or play. I'm always impressed with the forwards, those team members who move the ball into the net to score the winning goals.

Our society tells us that we need to be like forwards — goal-oriented. I have goals that I try to score each day, whether I'm finishing up tasks or cleaning up messes. But some days I feel as if I haven't accomplished anything, as if I'm not even in the game.

But consider another element of soccer known as an assist. In an assist, a player positions the ball so that his or her teammate can score. Assists can make a huge difference in winning or losing a game.

This concept give me a new perspective on how I keep score in my life. OK, maybe I didn't get my desk cleaned off, but I did call a lonely, elderly relative and cheered her up. Maybe I didn't get all my house and yardwork done, but I did visit a friend who was sick. While I scored no actual goals, I got two assists. My day certainly wasn't wasted.

Think about it. Many of Christ's deeds involved small kindnesses to the weak, the sick, and the poor. Many of these deeds could be classified as assists, but they added up to some impressive stats!

Maybe we keep track of the wrong things. In the overall total of our life's statistics, our assists may prove to be more significant and meaningful than our goals.

৵৶

Getting Ready

We went over the extensive list carefully: clothing, footwear, food, tickets, reservations. Aha! We found a serious omission threatening to ruin everything. I wrote down the vital item: a boutonniere.

It must be easier to mount an expedition to the Arctic than to dress a daughter for her first high school formal. When she finally left with her date, I slumped into a chair, exhausted.

Due to necessity, I discovered I had many untried talents: in turn, I became a fashion consultant and financier, a laundress, presser, seamstress, and valet; also a make-up artist, hairdresser, and general go-fer. And while I had not mastered any of these, I proved adequate for each job.

First, we shopped for dresses. My daughter's lithe, young form slid easily into both gossamer and slinky styles. It quite took my breath away to see her, my woman-child. The price tag was also heart-stopping, being somewhat more than my first apartment's monthly rent. Finally, she found something she loved. It fit almost perfectly; only slight tucks on the shoulder spaghetti straps were needed.

"This is my dress," she announced.

The flouncy dress shimmered; so did her face.

Next, of course we shopped for undergarments and shoes. We headed out of the familiar athletic shoe area to the one with little leather flats. Boxes later, we found a suitable pair, just before we wore out the salesman.

My daughter wisely borrowed a coat and bag, and then the outfit was complete.

The evening of the big event, I tried a new plastic gizmo to create a French bun. "Only a few easy minutes," the package promised. After several aborted attempts, I finally got the hang of it and secured the bun with huge pins and a heavy coat of hair spray.

She finished her make-up and we got her zipped up just as her date arrived; but some last minute primping left him in that traditionally awkward moment with us, "the parents." His young face glistened with anxiety as he clutched a corsage behind him.

At last, though, she made her appearance. Her date began breathing again, but I didn't. She was prettier than I've ever seen her. The French bun gave her face elegant angles; the short dress showed off curves never revealed in jeans and tees.

She smiled. She was truly lovely, and her date's goofy grin confirmed his delighted surprise.

But I saw something else. Was it her attitude, or did I just glimpse the future? I wiped a few tears as they left the house. I swear, truly, for a fraction of a second, I saw the self-assured professional woman she wants to become.

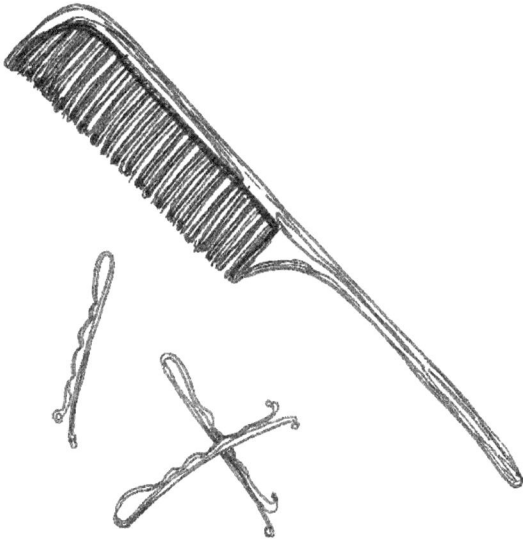

ॐॐ

On
Gratitude

To Count Our Blessings

Give us, O Lord, thankful hearts
which never forget your goodness to us.
Give us, O Lord, grateful hearts
which do not waste time complaining.
--St Thomas Aquinas

Dear Lord,

Hi, it's me. Yeah, things are going crazy around here again—like usual. I've got important project deadlines to meet, several concerts to sing, and the house is a mess. Christmas cards and shopping? You've got to be kidding. I may have to give everyone an IOU this year at the rate I'm going. No, I'm just not ready for Christmas.

Is there any way you could delay Christmas until, say, January 10th or so? It's the first clear spot I've got on my calendar.

What's that? I didn't quite hear you. Just a minute—let me turn off the music and the TV. Hmmm—let me silence my phone while I'm at it. I've talked with so many telemarketers lately that I could write my own catalog. There, that's better.

Now let me sit down and close my eyes for just a
moment.

Oh, this is so much better! Doing nothing but
talking with you feels simply delicious — a stolen
moment of time in a too-busy season. I can actually
feel your presence in the silence — it's quiet, but
powerful — your mute music washing around me
and through me. My addled mind is clearing
already, as if a bad cold suddenly faded away,
leaving a wholeness I'd nearly forgotten.

I can hear you now — you say you love me. I
feel your hug as if it were two strong arms gently
holding me. I feel comforted.

Thank you, Lord, I'm at peace now. I guess
you can go ahead and let Christmas come on its
normal date. Even if I don't have the trimming and
trappings in place, you reminded me of what is most
important: that you love the world, that you gave us
the precious gift of Jesus. The rest simply doesn't
matter.

ॐॐ

A Very Belated Thank You

Dear Great Aunt Nina,

You died in 1978. It seems so long ago. I was in my mid-twenties, busy getting my own life together, too busy to ask you how you were so successful in living yours. And you were phenomenally successful—born in 1890, you managed to get a master's degree in education at a time when it was difficult to find a college that even admitted women. And then, when you could have taught anywhere, you worked in an inner city school in Saginaw, Michigan, giving disadvantaged children a solid start in life.

You were like a second grandmother to that side of the family, involved with my brother, sister, and me as we grew. What I remember most was how interested you were in everything we did, and how wonderful your letters were. A letter you wrote describing my wedding is one of my favorite keepsakes.

A few years ago, another relative gave me an

old book before he died. As I opened the tooled leather cover, I instantly recognized your flowing script, alongside the handwriting of others, as it graced the lined, fragile pages. You and your friends and cousins recorded a fascinating account of camping experiences in the uncertain years before World War I. Did you really run around the woods in your bloomers? Did the boys really collapse the girls' tent at midnight? Did your sister—my grandmother—pine loudly for a beau with a car, which was a luxury and a novelty at the time? I marveled at your youth, your exuberance and the clear way you expressed yourself. You inspired me to try to write similar journals for my church's youth, telling the silly as well as the sane parts of youth tours. From there, I tried my hand at short stories and poems, and lately, a novel.

Someday, I hope to do your summer fun justice, and memorialize you and the other cousins in an historical novel. But for now, I want to say thank you for caring about me, and for giving me a template to live by. I hope I can measure up to it.

❧

Also by L. Phillips Carlson:

Little Christmases (short stories for the holidays)

Is holiday prep driving you nuts? You need a break! This little book of short stories is just for you — to laugh a bit and remind yourself that holidays don't always go as planned.

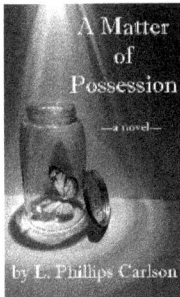

A Matter of Possession (a novel)

A dead co-worker, a rich woman's murder, and a stolen, rare butterfly collection —

New P.I. Joe Shurjack has a hard enough time taking on these strange cases. Then the ghost of his flirtatious coworker manifests and takes over his wife's body. She soon makes demands — ones that will cost Joe dearly.

Winner of 2015 New Mexico-Arizona Book Award, Science Fiction/Fantasy

Both books are available for Kindle and other devices; also in paperback at Amazon.com and other fine bookstores.

Previously Published List:

Original versions of the following were previously published in:

"Mended" — *The Upper Room*, Feb. 1998
"Letting Go" — *Asbury Trails*, Dec. 2010
"Wild Hair" — *The Raintown Review*, Jun. 1998
"F/X" — *Asbury Advent Devotional*, Dec. 1995
"Harbinger" — *Evangel*, Apr. 5, 1998
"Shadows and Light" — *Asbury Trails*, Oct. 1996
"Clean Sweep" (as "Clean and Crass") — *Asbury Trails*, Jan. 1996
"One Wrong Note" — *Asbury Trails*, Mar. 2004
"Close to Home" — *Asbury Trails,* Apr. 1997
"Listening to Your Father" — *Asbury Trails*, June 2008
"One of Those 'God Things'" — *Asbury Trails*, Sept. 2007
"Brown Jello" — *Asbury Trails*, Dec. 2007
"Keeping Statistics" — *Devo'zine*, Sept/Oct. 1998
"To Count Our Blessings" — *Asbury Trails*, Dec. 2002
"A Very Belated Thank You" (as "Dear Great Aunt Nina") — *Asbury Trails*, Dec. 2003

About the author

L. Phillips Carlson has more than 130 published articles, short stories and poems to her credit, most under a different pen name. Her short novel, *A Matter of Possession*, won the 2015 New Mexico-Arizona book award for Science Fiction and Fantasy. She also worked as a copy editor for a group of nationally-distributed magazines, wrote and edited a local newsletter for a decade, and penned an award-winning church history. When not writing, Ms. Carlson travels widely, sings in a symphonic chorus, and tends to various members of her family. She lives in sunny New Mexico with her retired-engineer husband in a pueblo-style home they designed themselves.

Website:
http://lphillipscarlson.com

Author page:
www.amazon.com/author/lphillipscarlson